BEFORE
THE
SCHOOL
BELL
RINGS

by Carol B. Hillman

Published by
PHI DELTA KAPPA EDUCATIONAL FOUNDATION
Bloomington, Indiana

Book design by Peg Caudell
Photograph credits:
Claire Yaffe - Pages 7, 20, 23, 34, 39, 55, 61, 66, 69
David M. Ruetschlin - Page 15
Vladimir Bektesh - Pages 27, 63

Library of Congress Catalog Number 95-67071
ISBN 0-87367-476-6
Copyright © 1995 by Carol B. Hillman
Bloomington, Indiana

PREFACE

Befor *the School Bell Rings* is for all people who love children, for everyone whose life significantly touches the life of a young child.

This book is for the individuals who make a difference in the initial education of young children — parents, step-parents, guardians, grandparents, childcare providers, friends, neighbors, and, of course, preschool teachers and other educators. Caring adults want all children's early years to be filled with healthy and joyful experiences. And this book will help caregivers make the best decisions for and about young children in the early childhood years before the start of formal schooling.

The education of young children is complex and dynamic. Readers who understand this view will find *Before the School Bell Rings* to be a source of ideas, advice, and, I hope, inspiration. I have written this book for those who believe that it takes far-reaching, collaborative efforts to educate young children well.

If this book is to be helpful to these diverse readers, then a common language is essential. With this in mind, I use the word *caregiver* to identify anyone involved in caring for a child or children. Sometimes suggestions or activities will be limited to one or two particular groups of caregivers, for example, to parents or guardians or to childcare providers. In those cases, I specifically identify the intended reader. Also, in an effort to address all children without bias and yet keep the text simple, I use the pronouns *she* and *he* in alternate chapters. But the information applies to both girls and boys, unless specifically noted.

Before the School Bell Rings will help caregivers:

- Learn how to enhance their powers of observation.
- Know each child as a unique individual.
- Discover ways to build trust between children and adults and between non-parent caregivers and parents.

- Design aesthetically pleasing, intellectually stimulating, safe, and comfortable learning environments.
- Understand and respect the importance of children's play.
- Explore the role of communication between caregiver and child and its significance to the learning process.
- Evaluate childcare facilities and staff.

Through numerous examples, I hope to energize readers. My goal is to encourage all caregivers to be positive thinkers and positive advocates for high-quality, nourishing, and empowering early childhood experiences and education. Much of what happens in children's lives before the school bell rings shapes their learning and emotional development throughout their years of formal schooling.

Carol B. Hillman
May 1995

TABLE OF CONTENTS

INTRODUCTION

"A family is what you feel," said the New York City schoolboy in a quiet voice.

Two or more people make up a family, any two people at all. Gender, age, nationality, and relatedness by birth are not significant factors. Rather, layer upon layer of devoted, caring, and spirited interactions, one with another, are what count. The intimacies of talk and silence, the sideward glances, and the nods of approval or subtle shakes of the head — those things shape a family's communication. Being part of a family is a lifelong tie, and it defines an individual.

The most powerful influence on a child is his family — especially during the early, formative years before the start of schooling. If a child is part of a "happy" family, he will most likely feel "at home" with his family. He will know what to expect, what he must do to hear his praises sung, and what he must do to steer clear of criticism and stay out of trouble.

The family is where the impulsive toddler learns that he must hold on tightly to an adult's hand when crossing a street. The toddler recognizes that his parents or caregivers insist on holding his hand because they love him and want to keep him safe. That loves comes through the held hand and "feels like family."

The family is home base, where the child dares to be himself and daily, sometimes hourly, tests the ground. It is where Joey pleads to stay up 30 minutes longer because "Lamar's mom always lets him." It is where Joey's dad says: "No, I won't buy you a cap gun because I don't believe in guns." In a family the child learns how to treat other people by carefully, constantly watching and listening to what is going on around him. He learns that how other people treat him is a consequence of how he acts, and he begins to shape his actions in order to influence the reactions of others.

Each child comes into the world with a given set of characteristics: certain talents, strengths, and frailties. As the child grows, he becomes all that he was born with and all that happens to him. Thus the formative early years are critical years, when traits of character are influenced and when young children gather and develop a strong sense of themselves and others. They begin to form a view of the world.

The very minute that the child enters the family, everything changes for the adult family member(s). For the new parent in particular, quite suddenly, there is a whole new focus. The home takes on new energy, vitality, and identity. At the same time, a new messiness may appear. Things are not as ordered or as clean as they once were. There are new and persistent sounds and smells. Sleep is interrupted. Routines change. And new "things" — a bassinet, a changing table, a diaper pail, etc. — claim their space.

Being a parent requires endless patience and tolerance for interruption and ambiguity. But the most effective parents do not forget to schedule time and space for themselves. Tired by a stressful day, they still find ten minutes to kick off their shoes, close their eyes, and lean back in a comfortable chair. Good parenting requires time for reflection. From reflection comes new insights.

Parents must come to terms with family traditions. What traditions should parents pass on to their children? Every family has traditions, simple ones and complex ones: pepperoni and black olive pizza every Friday night; calling Grandma on Sunday mornings at 10 o'clock; candles and one tall sparkler on chocolate birthday cakes; homemade strawberry ice cream on the Fourth of July; church services on Christmas Eve; hugs and kisses all around before bedtime.

Many traditions and practices in family life spring from deep convictions. But for all parents, much new learning also takes place — often as parents react "on the spot" to situations and events that center on the child. There is not always time to call Grandma or a trusted friend to seek advice. Thus parents decide how late Joey can stay up and whether Uncle David's gift of a shiny toy gun is acceptable based on convictions, traditions, and the dynamics of the moment.

Hard as it may be, parents need to be consistent in their interactions with young children. Joey may complain that he has "the meanest parents in the world," but he benefits from consistency and structure. Those elements make for stability and trust, and they make the family a safe, predictable place. Children need structure and support so that they can stand up tall and have strong walls off which to bounce or against which to push.

A child needs to know unconditional love from his family every day. The values and traditions that Joey takes from his family will color and shape the rest of his life. Questions that he may feel only subconsciously often are answered by his family experiences. Will people treat me fairly? How can I show that I'm angry? If a job is difficult, what do I do — give up or keep at it? Does it feel good to do things for other people? When things do not go my way, do I blame someone else or try to find a better way?

Joey also needs to learn about family and personal responsibilities. Being part of a family rightfully makes demands on him. The normal, sometimes difficult, give and take of family life provides many such learning opportunities. The seemingly eternal "pick up your clothes before you go out to play" and the continual "just use your eyes and don't touch anything when we visit Aunt Nancy" are simple examples. A child needs both unconditional love and responsibility to find a balance in life.

Joey must discover a jumble of feelings and learn how to deal with each one. There are the feelings of being cared for, such as those he associates with being fed his favorite egg noodles or rice and beans. There is the warm and playful feeling of being taken to the neighborhood park to make a "gorgeous" birthday cake of sand with twigs for candles for his best friend, Maria. There is the sadness of being sent to his room for calling Chai "stupid poo-poo head." And there is anger when his friend, Chester, cannot come out to play, and Joey rips three pages from his favorite book in frustration.

"A family is what you feel." Family is the very core of who we are. The "happy" family recognizes that give-and-take is an essential quality. The "happy" family trusts one another, and each member deals fairly with the others. They treat each other with genuine respect. In such families the members care deeply for one another; they nourish and succor one another so that all members can live their lives in fulfilling ways. Family relationships set the stage for a child's first endeavors and future development. A child's family is the first environment. How a family creates that environment helps to determine how the child will interact with and within future environments, such as the school.

The chapters that follow discuss how the young child's surroundings can be shaped and what might productively happen there. Readers will find suggestions about play and learning, communication, television and videos, and the outdoors and how to develop surroundings that support and nurture a child's development.

The chapters that follow are designed to stimulate the thinking of all caregivers: parents, guardians, child-care providers, teachers — whoever would help to shape the life of a child. In the broadest sense, all of these caregivers are "family."

CHAPTER ONE

CHILD'S PLAY

Doris sits atop a stack of three wooden chairs. A red-and-white dishtowel is tied around her neck. She is "reading" a magazine upside down while her friend, Amir, is fixing her hair. Amir is all thumbs at getting Doris' deep brown hair to stay in the pink plastic rollers at his pretend beauty parlor.

Robert stands with his right leg bent in front of his left. He twirls a lemon-yellow nylon scarf above his head. A red bandanna, folded in a triangle, covers the front of his shirt on his puffed-out "manly" chest. Robert is rounding up a herd of horses on the ranch.

Shanna and Okye sit side-by-side on two plastic, upended milk crates. Their white hardhats are pushed back off their foreheads. Their scuffed tan work boots have come untied. Shanna has just opened her lunch box and offered Okye a drink from her thermos. Shanna and Okye are two construction workers taking a lunch break.

All of these children have one thing in common. They are actively and enthusiastically learning about the world around them. They all are deeply engrossed in the art of play. Through play they are learning what they can do easily and what is frustrating. Doris is learning to be patient. She is finding out that "getting beautiful" takes a lot of time. Amir is learning that, for him, setting hair is hard. It makes a person mad when the rollers won't stay in place.

Robert is finding out that he must keep a certain rhythm to "rope" his horses. He is discovering that ranch work is really tiring when you have a dozen horses to corral.

And Okye and Shanna are learning that it feels good to have a work buddy and that sharing a lemonade on the job makes all the hard work worthwhile.

Young children are born ready to learn. They are passionate in their quest to take on new knowledge and understanding. They have a driving need to make sense of the world in which they and those for whom they care most deeply live. They are eager, even aggressive explorers. They must touch every object within their reach. They must turn things over and inside out. They have to smell the contents of the vanilla bottle as they are making sugar cookies. They are transformed when they hear the soft squeaks of the contented guinea pig that they hold in their lap. They are filled with joy when they watch the snow covering their sidewalk. They can't wait to taste the piping hot cookies they have just made — immediately — even if their fingers get burned a bit.

Young children see small details that adults may miss. A young toddler is fascinated by a dust ball that she plucks from the hardwood floor. A tiny ant crawling over the kitchen table delights her roving eye. Just as writer Leo Lionni's small mouse, Frederick, gathered sun rays, colors, and words for the long winter days ahead, very young children gather and store impressions, feelings, and memories before their words appear. These impressions compose a colorful patchwork quilt that helps children understand their place in the world.

QUESTION TIME

Young explorers and gatherers pose questions ceaselessly. "Why was Mr. McGregor so mad at poor Peter Rabbit?" "What's wrong with walking in the puddles when I love the splash they make?"

Children's endless questions allow them to seek adult interpretations for the flood of information that washes over them. An adult can sort things out for a child. An adult can make order and meaning of the sea of new experiences and impressions. Children also need to understand where you are coming from. They need to know the reasons why you think the way you do so

that they don't accept things by blind obedience or, conversely, feel moved to rebel.

Every question a child asks is a real inquiry and needs an answer. But it is not just the answer that is valuable. Sometimes simply taking time to answer a child's question is as important as the answer. Answering a child's question is saying without words, "I value you as a person. I value how you think and what you want to know."

Questions connect people, especially adults and children. Children want and need to be connected to the adults they love. Often, in fact, it is the connection that is the real issue for them. Children can't bear to feel pushed aside. They quickly wilt with hurt. They long to be valued people each day, from the moment they awaken until they are tucked into bed again at night.

And the questions can start early. At 7:45 a.m., when everyone is rushing to get out the front door on time for school and work, Sheila asks, "Why does Uncle Richard only see Brad and Timmy on Sundays?" Parents may be tempted to say, "Let's talk about it later" or "I can't take the time to explain right now. Don't you see I'm running late?" But if a question is not answered when it is asked, an intangible "something" is lost. The moment cannot be fully recaptured. Sometimes, however, a parent can buy some time by saying, "You have asked a really important question, and I am going to think about how to answer that." Then it is the parent's responsibility to raise the question again with the child, and to answer it.

Another way to keep track of important questions that cannot be answered on the spur of the moment is to keep a special question notebook. Placing the notebook in the kitchen makes it handy to write down questions that need to be answered later. And writing down a question gives it importance. The act of putting her question in writing assures Sheila that later there will be time to talk.

Of course, there will be questions that are beyond us. Some call for knowledge that parents or other caregivers don't possess; others are unanswerable. "How does the rain know when to stop?" "Why are dandelions yellow?" "What does a cricket eat?" In many cases, the best answer is, "I have often wondered about that, too," or simply, "I don't know."

Joining in a child's journey of discovery is an affirming parenting — and teaching — endeavor. Caregivers can use reference books or plan a trip to the library for a small research project. Together, adult and child can pour over the encyclopedia or start a computer search. Caregivers need to encourage questions because children learn by being encouraged to think, to wonder, and to dream about the simple and the complex in life.

PLAY PROVIDES ANSWERS

Seeking answers is one important reason why children play. Play shapes a young child's world. Through play a child weaves an understanding of what the world is like.

Playing with a stuffed toy dog, Jim can gently pat and stroke its fur, at the same time correctly learning how to treat his family's real dog. Meredith can pick a bouquet of wild asters and learn about the gift of flowers. Through play a child can become anybody or anything she wants, a handsome trapeze artist performing for the queen or a roaring lion on the jungle floor. Liz learns that she has an excellent sense of balance as she nimbly walks across the balance beam, being the tightrope walker. Isaiah feels a surge of power as he gives his deepest roar, being the undisputed jungle king.

Play as the learning medium for young children is different from standard classroom practice. The learning comes in a roundabout way through what is handled and what is done. Play, or exploration, is the intention; learning is the unintended outcome. For example, Okye and Shanna build the Empire State Building using wooden building blocks. They enjoy exploring the blocks' textures and weights. They experiment with balance. In the process, they learn that a tall building must start from a firm foundation.

In another situation, Manuel, dressed with a blue policeman's hat, directs traffic on a busy "street." Manuel learns that he must use hand signals and a whistle when he wants drivers to stop. Ari grabs a tie and jacket, stuffs a copy of the newspaper in his pretend briefcase, and rushes off "to work," replaying his father's actions of that morning. Sam and Carrie pretend to flip flapjacks for the farm workers before they go out to pick corn. Martha sits in a rocking chair, cuddling her babydoll, and "reading" her the story of *The Very Hungry Caterpillar.** Angie Lee is being a teacher and says in an authoritative voice, "Just forget about going outside until this mess is put away."

Many adults view such vignettes as merely "child's play" and disregard their importance. Of course, such activities *are* child's play — and that's the point. Child's play is how young children learn about the world. Therefore, it is imperative that caregivers understand this process of playing/learning and actively support the right of children to learn in this appropriate way.

Following are several ways to encourage and support healthy, productive children's play:

- Provide intriguing props.
- Make spaces for children that invite play.

---

*For the reader's convenience, all children's books mentioned throughout *Before the School Bell Rings* are listed in the "Favorite Children's Books" section of Chapter 4. That section begins on page 47.

- Join in children's play when invited.
- Urge children's extended families to visit their play spaces.
- Discuss the importance of play with other adults in a child's life.

Play is different for different ages. Just as the physical development of the child usually proceeds along known lines, the play pattern of a child often proceeds in a predictable way. An infant begins by discovering her fingers and toes and what her body is all about. Infants are self-absorbed. But soon enough, the infant laughs at peekaboo and reaches out to grasp at the mobile hanging over her crib.

As she grows, her world grows with her. She begins to crawl and to explore new areas. The kitchen cabinets become a treasure trove. Pots, pans, bowls, and wooden spoons are orchestrated. Plastic storage containers are stacked into towers. Objects take on meaning: a small bowl can fit into a larger one.

From playing beside one another, young children begin to play *with* one another. At first, toddlers do not necessarily play together, yet they learn from one another. They are ever watchful, taking in a multitude of sights and sounds. The toddler, at this stage, is engaged in parallel play. Usually in a child's third year a new awareness comes bursting forth. Brian discovers that two people can move a wooden ladder more easily than one person. He finds that rolling a huge snowball takes a bunch of helpers. With more helpers the snowball rolls more smoothly, and it's also a lot more fun. These are some of the pleasures that Brian discovers about cooperative play.

This later stage of children's play is readily evident in a room filled with boisterous, energetic four- and five-year-olds. The "doctor," "nurse," and "ambulance driver" cluster together for a serious talk about what needs to happen next. The "doctor" has her stethoscope draped around her neck, "the nurse" has bandages clutched in his hands, and the "ambulance driver" bends low over the imaginary steering wheel as the ambulance races to the hospital. The "patient" lies behind them, rigid, with tightly closed eyes. These four children are playing as a unit. Imagining themselves to be en route to the emergency room of the hospital, they are enacting a crisis situation. Perhaps the situation arose from something they saw on television or perhaps from a real-life drama. Whatever the impetus, they are deeply absorbed in sociodramatic play. Through their play the children are becoming familiar with life events. They are, in many ways, rehearsing for adult life by striving to comprehend the world through reenactment.

Play also is the way that children learn what it is like to be in charge, to be responsible. Through play, young children gain a sense of power as they make "big-time" decisions. When Jeanne puts on a wide-brimmed straw hat, three strands of colored beads, and fire-engine red, high-heeled shoes, she has a definite mission in mind. With her long, scribbled list in hand, Jeanne is going to the market. Making out that list, which is illegible to the adult eye, is part of learning to make decisions. That scribbled list may note that it is time to buy another jar of chunky peanut butter, because the jar in the cupboard is almost empty. Making the list also helps Jeanne connect how food comes from the grocery store to the kitchen table.

Play as an organizing force lends form to children's lives. As in a well-written story, play events have a beginning, a middle, and an end. In children's play, there are roles to undertake and to learn about. Children need to learn how to lead and how to follow. When Sam is "the driver" of the bus, he has to decide whether to head for the St. Louis Zoo or the puppet show at Mount Grace church. He must see that everyone is seated comfortably. He must see that all seat belts are fastened. All of that is part of being in charge and taking the leadership role. On the other hand, if

Sam is a passenger in the bus, he must do as the driver says. He needs to sit down and make sure his seat belt is fastened. He needs to be careful not to push any other passenger. And he must listen to the directions that the "bus driver" calls out. All of that is part of the follower's role.

There are other concepts that children learn through cooperative play, such as negotiation, that can be difficult. When three children build an airport control tower, they must plan its size and shape. Jane hauls blocks to the building site. Caroline insists that the tower must have two large square windows. Jamel is adamant for three rectangular ones. Working together, children learn that there are times when they must change their desired plans.

Negotiation also underlies taking turns. Building with blocks dictates a certain rhythm. Not everyone can build at the same time. And so builders learn to respect this rhythm and to synchronize their moves. Jane, Caroline, and Jamel must share materials, take turns placing blocks, and negotiate the shape of the structure. In doing so, they also build an understanding of cooperation.

Learning how to make competent decisions takes much time and practice, but how empowering it is for children! When Jennifer decided that the gray-and-white rabbit at her childcare center merited the name "Cloudy," all her four-year-old classmates cheered and clapped. What a great feeling that gave Jennifer! Making good decisions builds children's self-esteem in two ways. First, the power to make decisions is affirming. It says to the child, "You are a capable person." Second, good decisions bring praise, which validates the child's self-worth.

Decisions, and the events that surround them, proceed from simple to more complex as children grow.

Asking three-year-old Juanita if she is making strawberry shortcake or chocolate cake when she is whipping up a bowl of soapsuds is in keeping with her age. A five-year-old can choose from a more extensive menu. Caregivers need to create many opportunities for children to practice making decisions — both those that involve imagination and those that involve real things. Melanie can decide if she wants to wear her old, patched blue jeans or her new, bright-green corduroys. She can decide if she wants french toast or cereal for breakfast.

At a childcare center each child needs to choose what she wants to do in the morning. Does she want to paint at the easel, help make applesauce, or work on the new floor puzzle of a pirate ship? A child can cast a vote on whether to make purple or blue play dough for the week. She can decide if she wants to feed the toad two or three mealworms — and if she will use the tweezers or be brave and pick up the worms with her fingers.

A natural partner of making decisions is solving problems, which takes many forms in children's play. For Luis, the problem may be to make purple paint. What colors must he mix? If Luis is allowed and encouraged to experiment, he will probably discover that he can solve his problem by mixing red and blue paint. One of the essential ingredients in children's play is being allowed time to explore and to experiment. Young children need time to think about problems and to try out possible solutions. They need many opportunities to make mistakes and to correct them.

Then they need time to put solutions to use and to practice new skills. After Elizabeth learns how to hold and use scissors, she needs many opportunities (and reasons) to cut paper and ribbon in order to gain proficiency and self-confidence in her new skills. Playtime should present children with events and activities that encourage observation, call for decisions to be made and problems to be solved, and require new skills to be developed and practiced. Playtime also should give children opportunities to talk about what they are learning and doing with adults and with other children. And some children need lots of extra time just to sit and think before they venture forth. Only then can children "put it all together" and perhaps add their own original twist.

TWO WORLDS

Young children live in two worlds, the world of reality and the world of fantasy. It is part of who they are, and it is part of their irresistible charm. Often, it seems, they live in both worlds simultaneously.

Children's belief in fantasy is unconditional. There are few other times of life when one can know such pure freedom. A simple, red plastic fireman's hat can turn three-year-old Maureen into a fierce fire fighter. A small piece of pink tulle can turn four-year-old Janet into a graceful ballerina.

Caregivers can enter into children's play either by invitation or, in some instances, by momentary inspiration. Children love to see an adult role play. An adult

can don a deerstalker cap and slink about with a magnifying glass, playing the great detective; the actions will delight children on a level that requires absolutely no knowledge of Sherlock Holmes. Their delight arises from seeing the grownup play.

In the same way, children invariably get a resounding laugh out of seeing a grownup put on a stethoscope and listen to Winnie the Pooh's heartbeat. And they learn a lesson in sympathetic understanding when the adult says, "Oh Pooh Bear, I'm so sorry to hear you fell off the swing. Do show me where it hurts." Such role playing helps Bill understand what adults do, and perhaps reminds him of what grownups have done with him when he didn't feel well. In moments like this, a child and an adult can feel closely connected.

Caregivers need not worry that children will remain in a "dream world" too long. Reality is always nearby. And as children mature, the world of fantasy diminishes as their contact with the real world increases.

Occasionally, the world of fantasy becomes troublesome. An example is the super-hero scenario in which fantasy has taken a giant leap. Super-hero fantasies are not neat and tidy like playing school or pretending to shop at a grocery store. Sometimes such fantasies are filled with high emotion and rambunctious physical, often aggressive, activity. What is the attraction of Superman, the Power Rangers, or the Ninja Turtles for young children? In part, the answer is that youngsters are seldom in control. They are told what to do and when and how to do it. The super hero symbolizes power — the power that they wish they had to be like adults and to make things happen. While some children respond negatively to the super-hero fantasy and become overly aggressive or destructive, most children can play the super hero within reasonable bounds. For these children, the super-hero fantasy helps them to be more accepting of themselves as they visualize their power.

Children's play is primarily self-directed. For this very reason there are few rules to follow. Children set the boundaries that feel right to them. This allows for considerable freedom of expression. Because of this glorious sense of freedom, play can be original, inventive, and fresh. It is critical that caregivers respect this premise and let children play in their own way. Let Paula shout, "Get your little tush in here if you know what's good for you." Let Asa stuff his pants with the doll blanket so that he can look nine months pregnant.

Caregivers can use children's play as time to observe and record how spirited youngsters think and feel. Observing children at play helps the adults in their lives fit together the pieces of the patchwork quilt. Adults at home or in a childcare center always have mountains of things to do. There are always crumpled clothes to pick up, dirty dishes to wash, or blocks and puzzles to put away. Adults in the presence of children can be in motion all day long. But just as there is wisdom in pausing to answer a child's question, there also is wisdom in sitting quietly and watching a child at play. And here again, by giving a child undivided attention, the adult is saying without words, "I like to watch what you are doing because I believe in you."

CHAPTER TWO

A LEARNING AND PLAYING ENVIRONMENT

Young children are like tuning forks attuned to life's vibrations. Their senses act as antennae, and they respond to the environmental "music" by absorbing the rhythms, the words, and the notes of each melody. They react to new recordings as well as to old refrains.

Young children encounter many environments: their home, the childcare center, a neighborhood bakery, a yellow school bus. Each place conveys a feeling and tells its own story. And each place helps the child to grow by adding fresh sensations and experiences.

But deliberately creating a learning environment for young children can be best accomplished on the basis of sound educational philosophy. Children learn most effectively in a place where love abounds and people feel connected. They learn best in a place where they don't feel rushed, where they are cradled in stretches of time. They learn best where they feel safe and can ask for help. And they learn best where they are mentally and physically challenged by new ideas and activities.

A child's world should be filled with light, color, and chatter. Objects might include:

- a conch shell to listen to the singing of the sea;
- pillows to settle into and listen to *Mr. Rabbit and the Lovely Present* and other stories;
- paint and paper for making broad strokes of bluejay blue;
- ingredients to make new foods, like Irish soda bread, to be tasted for the very first time;

- a swing on which to practice pumping and a patch of grass for hopping on one foot;
- a magnifying glass to examine maple leaves.

A child's world should be plain and simple but filled with a multitude of everyday things. It should be a clearly defined space so that children can see and sense the order. A child's world calls for a sense of order so that choices are easy to make. But it also must be a space with "things" that invite imagination and investigation. Children's spaces should draw children in because the spaces are intriguing, mysterious, and beautiful.

Caregivers must be concerned with aesthetics. Children's rooms at home and in childcare centers should be bathed in sunlight. They should be well-scrubbed places in which the furnishings and objects are kept in good repair. Spaces should dance with color, with children's paintings adorning the walls. Caregivers can bring the beauty of nature indoors by gathering bittersweet, pine boughs, and forsythia in vases and wreaths.

Perhaps the best way to think about children's spaces is to try to see them through children's eyes. Commercial artwork and cartoon figures are merely decorative; they do not represent children's inner thoughts. In their place should be children's work: their paintings and collages, papier mâché structures, mobiles, and "sculptures" of scrap wood and found objects. Rather than slick commercialism, it is the rich artistic expression of children that should visually bring their rooms to life.

In the words of Louis Malaguzzi, children should be "the authors of their own learning"* Parents and other

---

*Malaguzzi, Louis. *The 100 Languages of Children: The Reggio Emilia Approach to Early Childhood Education.* Reggio Emilia, Italy, A.C.M., 1987.

caregivers merely set the stage. They design the back-drop, provide the costumes, and bring in the props. They give cues when they are needed. Each day they raise the curtain. No performance is quite the same as the previous one. But what is constant — and must be constant — is a trust in children to learn and grow at every opportunity.

WELL-APPOINTED PLAY SPACE

Children need both change and routine. Childcare spaces, mirrored more modestly in home spaces for children, should be designed along the philosophical lines expressed above. Following are some practical applications for a block play area:

- Provide blocks that are clean, ordered, and labeled. A well-appointed play space will contain several hundred blocks in various sizes and shapes.

- Provide accessories to complement block con-structions. Such accessories include toy sailboats, tugboats, airplanes, dumptrucks, bulldozers, trains, ambulances, fire engines, and traffic signs. Baskets of wooden people with different color skins, young and old, doing different types of jobs also complement the building blocks, as do toy farm animals and wild animals. Doll-size furniture can be provided to replicate a home.

- Include a basket of cardboard scraps, markers, masking tape, and other craft supplies that can be used to "customize" building projects.

- Use colored tape to mark off an area in front of the shelves as a "No Building Zone" to give access to the shelves. But give ample space to the build-ing area.

Making a well-appointed play space such as this block-building area sends an unspoken message that such play is valued and important. Even quite young children will understand this message.

Caregivers also should watch what happens in the play space. They need to watch to see if Doreen is still hesitant to enter into group play. They need to be ready to intervene if Liam gets angry and is about to punch Carlos in the arm. But they also need to be available to pose questions that may spark children's thought. For example, "How do people get to the top floor?" or "Where can I park my car?" can help children think about the nature of buildings and how people interact with structures.

Another important area should be set aside for dramatic play. Children need to act out a variety of real-life and imaginary episodes as a way of making sense of the world. Therefore, a dramatic play area needs to be visually alive. It needs clean, colorful, well-repaired clothes hung on hangers or hooks; hats of all descriptions, ties, and capes; and footwear from work boots to fancy party shoes. There should be white jackets for

doctors and aprons for chefs. There should be pocket-books and briefcases, lens-less glasses, shaving brushes, a cane and crutches, and sparkly jewelry. There should be many symbols of adult life so that children can try them on and in so doing "try on" the adult role that accompanies the symbol.

The dramatic play area also should be a living entity, a dynamic and changing place that can be what children yearn to have it be. Caregivers need to listen to see if a new pizza parlor should open its doors or if the farmers are about to harvest their corn. Caregivers need to be scavengers, collectors of symbols, so that the scenes and props can be changed accordingly. And, as in the block-building area, caregivers need to be near the dramatic play area so that they can hear what is going on and respond appropriately.

Dramatic play can spill out into the building area and other play spaces. It should not be confined. If a "mommy and daddy" want to push their baby in a carriage, then they need room to stroll. If the milk carrier wants to deliver milk, he must visit his customers "all over town." In some respects, the rooms where children play are replicas of the outside (real) world. But it is also true that, for the children, the rooms where they play *are* their real world for now.

SCIENCE FOR YOUNG CHILDREN

Science for young children is many things: watching and listening, smelling and tasting, holding things, and looking at changes. It is puzzling out what has happened and thinking about what is coming next. Above all, science for young children is an attitude.

Just like blocks and dramatic play, science is an important focus for play. It also can be part of many play spaces. Science includes preparing a habitat for a toad, digging up earth and soft green moss, and baking oatmeal cookies whose delicious smell hangs in every cranny of the room. Thus the science "space" embodies the attitude that allows children to catch a jumping cricket and let it tickle the palms of their hands or to bring a bowlful of snow inside to watch it melt.

Science centers on observation. Therefore, it can begin with a simple question, such as, "What's different in the room today?" This will send the small detectives on an exciting hunt. Noticing what is different has broad implications. It can heighten sensitivity to detail. It can evoke memory and invite comparison.

No formal curriculum is necessary for young children because science can be many things:

- observing how cream is made into butter by a lot of shaking in ice cold jars;
- making a "greenhouse" for a green bean seed using a plastic bag and a rubber band;
- watching a black swallowtail butterfly emerge from its chrysalis;
- feeding a pet guinea pig and finding out what it likes to eat.

Like spaces for building with blocks and acting out roles, space for science can be made in the home as easily as in a childcare center. The difference is merely a matter of scale. At home, a child still can hold and feed a guinea pig. He can brush its fur and watch the way his pet nibbles on parsley and tomatoes. Each week or two he can weigh the guinea pig and see how much it gains. He can delight in bathing the guinea pig in warm water and mild soap and then observe how different the animal looks when its hair is soaking wet and matted down. He can dry its hair with a hair dryer and a towel and make his pet "handsome" again.

Pets such as guineas pigs teach children important lessons about pet care, nutrition, animal activities — indeed, about life and death. Children learn that animals get sick, are taken to the vet, and most often get well. But they also learn that sometimes a beloved pet may die. They learn to be responsible. They learn how a living thing can depend on them. "Parenting" a pet is an effective learning activity, and there are many pets from which to choose. In addition to guinea pigs, dogs, cats, and other common pets, the following make good pets:

- frogs, toads, and chameleons;
- red efts and hermit crabs;
- rabbits, gerbils, and hamsters;
- African love birds, parakeets, and angel fish;
- crickets, meal worms, earthworms, and ants; and
- monarch, swallowtail, and painted lady caterpillars.

There are a multitude of available creatures and critters, each with its own lifestyle. Each can be exciting to watch and care for on a daily basis. By giving children opportunities to cultivate their powers of observation and to practice "parenting" skills, they come to know that they are trusted and needed in this world.

A LIBRARY CORNER

The library corner, whether in the childcare center or in the child's room at home, should be a haven, a quiet, relaxing place where the child can snuggle into books. The library corner needs a certain softness with textures and colors that wrap around one's shoulders. Soft music lends a soothing tone.

There are times when a child wants to be alone, and a library corner is a good place to get away from taking turns, sharing favorite toys, and being a cooperative soul. Time in a library corner is time to look at pictures, to ponder ideas, and to cuddle on comfortable pillows with Paddington Bear.

In other moments, the library corner is the place to hear a story read. Children grow to love books and stories by being read to. They relish pressing close to a caring reader and becoming part of that make-believe world.

Books create their own kind of magic. They bring words and pictures that enter a child's memory, and those memories grow and change with the child. But words and pictures also hold a promise because the child soon realizes that "Someday I, too, can learn to read."

Children's books should be displayed with their covers facing outward, unlike adult bookshelves that show only the spines of the books. Books are like friends, and children need to see their "faces." Making sure the books are displayed "face out" is important, as is putting the books at the child's eye level.

At home, ending the day with a bedtime story is a perfect opportunity for close bonding between parent and child. And telling a story can be a magical event. Parents who read or tell their children stories at bedtime soon will engender a reciprocal desire in the child. Few activities hold more charm than hearing a child tell a story or pretend to read from a storybook. But such activity also enlivens the child's sense of what a story is

and the importance of settings, characters, and actions. Good story sense is an important skill that naturally develops when children have opportunities to interact with stories in many ways.

CHILDREN'S ART

Finally, children's art should be a pervasive element in the learning and playing environment. Art is an expression of what children are feeling and thinking. And it plays a key role in learning, because it is the outward expression of children's impressions and understandings about the world around them.

Art is more than the creation of a product. Artistry continues long after the work is done in the arrangement, the spacing, and the placing of visual elements. But art should not be formally taught or isolated as a special time of day. Effective children's art is not about coloring books or other formulas. It is not about working with other peoples' ideas; it is about children's own ideas. And so helping children create their own works of art requires an openness to experimentation with many different materials.

A child might make his own interpretation of a robin's nest using mud, twigs, and fine grasses. His fashioning of a soft cushion for the eggs reveals his understanding of birds and nests. He gets to think like a robin, and this "thinking and doing" like a robin solidifies the learning. He can extend that learning by painting a picture of a robin pulling a fat earthworm from the ground, by constructing a papier mâché robin, or by making clay robin eggs and painting them blue.

Children's art is an investment in creative learning. For adult caregivers, it should be born of a respect for children's ideas and children's capacity to grow through experiences that put them in touch with the world. And, like books, science, dramatics, and other play, art enhances and expands the learning and playing environment for young children.

CHAPTER THREE

COMMUNICATION

"Why do butterflies fly?"

"How does a robin know where to find a worm?"

"Where does the water go when it goes down the drain?"

"What makes the streetlights go on at night?"

Young children are brimming over with ideas and questions. Often their questions come so rapidly that parents can hardly wait for bedtime so that they can enjoy some tranquil moments. But questions and musings are the core of motivation. They cause children to risk new experiences and to acquire new skills.

Communication between caregiver and child is essential to the child's development. The way that caregivers react to children's questions shape communication. Are caregivers enthusiastic about hearing the child's thoughts? Do caregivers focus attention on the child? Is the child encouraged to share ideas and to ask questions when her curiosity is raised? Often such communication serves to signal the child that her ideas are important because the significant adults in her life take time to respond to her. Thus the way caregivers respond to children needs to be deliberate and caring.

Children are quick to read the unsaid in adult communication. If a parent says, "Get upstairs and into bed before I count to three," the child does not miss the message that there will likely be a negative consequence for failing to go to bed immediately. "Did you ever hear of wiping your shoes off before you tramp mud on the living-room rug?" carries a very different connotation than, "Please wipe your shoes so that the mud isn't carried into the living room." Consequently, caregivers need to look at their own feelings that underlie communications. Such self-knowledge forms a foundation for effective care.

Sometimes such self-examination is focused by a child. When Robert says, "Angelo's dad is more fun than you," the parent or other caregiver must deal with his or her own vulnerability, but not at the expense of Robert's feelings. Rather than hurt or resentment, Robert's caregiver needs to ask why the child perceives Angelo's dad as "more fun." Perhaps the reason is inconsequential. On the other hand, it may point the way to improving communication.

Caregivers need to ask themselves difficult questions, such as, Who do I want to be? and How do I go about getting there? Caregivers, like all human beings, need dreams and ideals by which to live. They need to set goals for themselves and their relationships with others. They need to know what they do well and what they need to improve.

Attaining personal goals is an individual matter; but when caregivers set goals and strive toward them, it affects communication with young children. Adults who work with young children often adopt views about certain children that may unfairly limit those children. In many cases, these stereotypes arise from unresolved personal goals and misconceptions about the importance of communication among children and adults. If the caregiver thinks, "Ling is like a quiet little mouse, so I shouldn't expect much participation or enthusiasm from her," then the caregiver may not take time to draw Ling out and to encourage the child's social development.

If the caregiver thinks, "Alethaire is always in motion, stirring up the pot, waving her hand frantically at circle or meeting time, and constantly interrupting," then the caregiver may view Alethaire's enthusiasm and gregariousness as negatives instead of as the positive qualities that they are.

The caregiver's sense of self is reflected in interactions with children. The caregiver's attitude conveys what is possible; and for young children to flourish, that attitude should say that many things are possible. For shy Ling, that may mean waiting a few moments longer to give her ample time to gather her thoughts so that she can tell about her four new goldfish. For vivacious Alethaire, that may mean gently telling her to put her hand down so that Lionel can have a turn to speak. These actions help to build a reality of respect for each child.

POSITIVE FEEDBACK

Receiving positive feedback for their actions plays a big part in building children's self-esteem. Caregivers should acknowledge a child's good qualities and focus on their positive actions.

Children need specific examples of how they can earn praise, real and recent actions that the caregiver can point out. When Ria shows a generous nature, her mother can tell her how thoughtful it was to share her Halloween candy with her cousin, or her childcare teacher can tell her how kind she was to see that the rabbit had fresh water in its bowl. These specific compliments are more meaningful than just saying, "Ria, you are such a generous and kind child." Broad, general compliments can overwhelm a child. Ria might react by thinking, "There is no way I can always be generous and kind. What if I mess up, will they still think I'm wonderful? Maybe I should play it safe and just not do anything at all."

Parents and other caregivers also need to listen to other people who know and work with children, to hear positive statements about the children. When a teacher says that Talbert came for a visit and worked on a wooden astronaut puzzle for more than ten minutes until he figured it out, the parent should congratulate Talbert for his persistence and a job well done. When Grandpa calls to say that Ashton dug her own worms and even baited her own hook so she could catch "a big f'ounder," a parent or teacher can "piggyback" on the positive experience by telling Ashton how proud she must be of herself.

Parents and teachers also can use such positive information to expand their knowledge of the child and then can use that knowledge to create new learning experiences. Talbert can be challenged with other puzzles; Ashton can be given additional opportunities to assert her independence.

MODELING COMMUNICATION

Part of helping children become good communicators is being a role model. No matter what caregivers say at home or in a childcare center, chances are that little ears are listening — even when nearby children seem to be engrossed in their own activities. Most parents have had the experience of burning the toast and exclaiming, "Dammit, I can't believe I did that," only to hear their words echoed back to them from a little "witness" at some future time.

Good communication modeling begins by building trust. This process starts in infancy. When a mother feeds and changes her baby, she talks softly. She says, "You are the sweetest, most adorable baby in the whole wide world." When little Olga fusses and gets picked up and rocked, the caregiver makes soothing sounds in words and songs. And so children grow to know that communication — those words and sounds and faces and movements — connotes trust. The child trusts the adult to look after her needs for comfort, food, and care.

Young children continue to need to know that a parent or caregiver can be counted on. They need to know consistency and stability in their lives. Spencer feels good when he wakes up because he knows that orange juice, cereal, and toast are waiting for him each morning at the childcare center. Bertha looks forward to the weekend, knowing that her adored Granny Gran will be coming to play with her. When caregivers remember that Natalie always (for now) wants her milk in the purple plastic cup, that makes them more believable, more trustworthy.

The issues in the lives of toddlers and preschoolers are deeper. But the need for caregivers to build credibility through honest words and positive, consistent actions every single day does not diminish. By attending to good role modeling, caregivers build positive images that shape youngsters' lives. Children use that personal storehouse to decide how they will act.

LISTENING, TOO

Caregivers must be good listeners to truly be good communicators. In fact, just being attentive to a child's concerns often is the greatest part of what the child needs. For example, Eliot is part of a busy family with four rambunctious brothers and sisters all clamoring for attention. Sometimes, he needs time to be with just one person who will focus on him.

Eliot needs to see examples of good listening amid the hubbub of his busy family or the even busier child-care room. Thus responsible caregivers will be careful to model group listening and one-on-one listening for Eliot and to structure situations where Eliot can practice good listening with other children — and where Eliot also can be the center of attention as others listen to him.

Caregivers at home and elsewhere need somehow to be outfitted with special antennae to sense what is going on everywhere at all times. They need to have

ears that are trained to discern when Cory's voice is getting agitated and he needs a calming voice and soothing presence. Just as a good cook knows by subtle smells when the cornbread is *about* to burn, so caregivers need to pick up subtle aural cues to know when Cory is likely to "blow" and clobber Hal with a block.

Visual cues, of course, supplement good listening. Seeing Cory's reddening face and angry movements from across the room should nonverbally signal the observant caregiver that intervention would be prudent.

HELPING CHILDREN MAKE CHOICES

Another aspect of communication relates to teaching children to make choices. When three-year-old Mira is asked to clean up her room each evening before supper, the job should be made as simple as possible for her. The caregiver can model picking up toys, and Mira will imitate the model. The caregiver can help Mira choose three stuffed animals to put on the bed, and then show her how to put away the other ten in the toy box.

One task at a time makes the whole job easier, just as it does when Langston is asked to put his blocks away and, when that job is done, is asked to do something else. This procedure for young children is preferable to expecting them to remember and accomplish multiple tasks assigned all at once.

Giving children simple choices makes them better communicators. Choosing between red socks and blue ones lets a youngster feel in control and better able to express herself. This builds self-esteem.

Communication, to be effective, means that caregivers must train themselves to be observant and responsive. And to help children become effective communicators means modeling good communication for them — looking, listening, and speaking. Each time that a caregiver communicates with a child, it is part of a larger picture — part of the binding cord.

CHAPTER FOUR

WORDS AND BOOKS

uthor Maya Angelou once wrote, "I love the book and the look of words." Caregivers should strive to have children love words and books. How magical and empowering it is when children think in pictures engendered by lines like this one from Margaret Wise Brown's perennial favorite, *The Runaway Bunny:* "If you become a bird and fly away, I will be a tree that you come home to."

For young children to build images, caregivers first must give them images. Who can know a tree who has not seen a tree? Therefore, in choosing children's books it is important to seek works that also contain captivating illustrations. Ferdinand, the bull, who likes to sit quietly under the cork tree smelling the flowers; the very busy spider diligently spinning her web; Frederick, the small mouse, spouting forth his poetic words — these are radiant images. Such images capture children's hearts, and such experiences build excited anticipation so that they can hardly wait for story time.

When caregivers are successful in their choices of books, children eagerly scamper to the library corner to curl up with *Corduroy*. They almost leap into a father's lap for a bedtime story. Words, pictures, and books become so much a part of each and every day that children don't feel as though the day is complete until they have heard a favorite story.

CHOOSING THE BEST CHILDREN'S BOOKS

Before children learn to read for themselves, caregivers set a positive stage for reading by their sincerity and enthusiasm about books and stories. Those who would instill a love of books in children understand children's interests and spend time at the library or the bookstore, pouring over picture books, and deciding which ones to take home or to the childcare center. They bring *Gilberto and the Wind* because they have in mind a kite project for the children. They include Leo Lionni's *Swimmy* to remind the children about the importance of cooperation. They choose Jane Yolen's *Owl Moon* for its portrayal of a tender father-child relationship.

Caregivers should choose books suited to the age of their young listeners. Some books just won't do. Books that are too wordy make the children fidget because young children do not have long attention spans, nor can they yet follow an intricate story line. Books that are too frightening raise needless anxieties and may disrupt their sleep.

Each book should be so compelling that the reader can hardly wait to share it. Keeping a list of best-loved books, authors, and illustrators can be useful as a record of books worth a return visit.

At the end of this chapter, I have included a list of books that are especially effective for reading to and with young children. Most are simple stories with engaging illustrations. They are books that adults will enjoy as much as children do.

Choosing good books is not without an occasional problem. For example, children at a childcare center often bring books from home that they want the teacher to read to all the children. But teachers should not automatically take up such books. Sometimes, the child must be told, "I have looked over this book and don't feel it is a book that the whole group would be inter-

ested in hearing." However, it may be reasonable to read the book to only the child who brought it.

READING TO CHILDREN

One excellent practice that can be followed at home or in the childcare center is having story time each morning. When reading to an individual child or to a group of children, the activity does not need to be confined to a special "story place." Reader and listeners can move around the room (or sit under a tree outside), as long as there is ample space. Children in listening groups need a place that is comfortable and where they do not feel "squished together." They need to be able to wiggle and should not be expected to sit still with their hands folded in their laps.

Caregivers can create a more intimate story experience by sitting at the child's level when they read aloud. This practice says to the child, "We are sharing significant moments and we like to be near each other." At home or in the childcare center, reading a story with a child should be a calming time. Story time often serves as a change of pace, a settling down after some vigorous activity. But it also can set the stage for a new activity, such as when the children begin to make their kites after hearing *Gilberto and the Wind.*

Different types of stories should be read to children. Some stories help children learn about the world immediately around them by focusing on the here and now. Others transport them to distant lands and connect them with the wider world. As Kibi imitates the calls of birds in Taro Yashima's *Crow Boy,* children sense Kibi's relationship with the land he knows. They can translate that sense to feelings that they have about the land they know.

USING POEMS AND SONGS

Nursery rhymes and poems are a must for young children. The words paint pictures while the rhythms and rhymes make music. Many children's rhymes have been set to music, or children will sing simple rhymes using made-up tunes of their own. Children love hearing rhymes, poems, and songs over and over. Books of poems should have an honored place in children's lives, just as storybooks do. And caregivers need to read poems to children with all the drama of stories.

Children are natural poets. They use words in simple, engaging ways:

"I just want to see around."
"The sink burps."
"Hold tight to the trees at night, butterfly."
"There's no room for words, there's too much love inside."

Reading and singing can be further explored when caregivers encourage children to make up rhymes and songs. An example is this rhyme about the childcare center's guinea pig:

Sweet Potato is our guinea pig.
Please Sweetie, will you dance a jig?

Caregivers can extend this freedom of expression by writing down children's words to be saved and read again several times. Caregivers and children can make whole books of original rhymes and add them to the library shelf at home or at the childcare center.

Children need time to be absolutely silly. They delight in falling to the floor with laughter at their own jokes or rhymes. They need to appreciate themselves as authors. They need to feel the freedom to say what makes them laugh. By capturing their words in handmade books, caregivers validate the importance of their ideas and stories.

STORYTELLING IS SPECIAL

Caregivers can be the dramatic readers of storybooks and poetry, having children hushed and straining forward so that they don't miss a word — and that is a wonderful thing to do. However, as we read to children, there is a book between us, a prop, an object in motion as we turn one page and then the next. The presence of a book makes the connection between adult and child less direct, an interruption of intimacy that storytellers do not have.

Storytelling is a solo performance — no book, no pictures, no distractions. How often do readers of books hear the pleading voice: "But I can't see the pictures!" Storytellers make their own pictures, imaginary visions compounded of words, expressions, gestures, and tone of voice. The storyteller's eyes catch the eyes of each child and hold fast to their young imaginations.

Storytelling can begin with the retelling of a favorite book story, such as Esphyr Slobodkina's *Caps for Sale*, or with the recounting of a well-known tale, such as "Little Red Riding Hood" or "Goldilocks and the Three Bears." Then creative storytellers can progress to original stories, often drawing them from the everyday lives of the children. These stories can be about going to the store or making a cake, and fantasy elements can be introduced along with the realism of everyday events.

Children can be storytellers, too. Caregivers can let them start with something in their hands. Maki can talk about her prized red dumptruck and how she uses it to haul a hill of sand. Willie can bring in a picture of the

first pickerel he caught on Lake Winnebago and tell about his triumphal moment. Carver, the budding sportsman, can display his precious baseball cards and share his excitement about collecting.

Caregivers can record children's stories, either on audiotape or with pen and pad. Parents can collect the stories their children tell, and teachers in the childcare center can record stories to share with parents and other significant adults in the children's lives. Stories become a part of the collective memory of the classroom or the family.

Following is a sample story told by four-year-old Melissa:

The Seven Ducks

The seven ducks decided to go for a swim because they were bored sitting around on the land, eating, which they had been doing for a million days and nights.

They wanted to swim to the Bronx River. As they swam, they ate all the fish that they saw. Once they got to the Bronx River, they didn't stop because they wanted to swim all the way around the world and see everything they could see. But when they got to Hawaii, they stopped. It was so sunny. They wanted to get a suntan, which they did. When that was done, they went home, where they took a nap.

The End

CREATING A BOND BETWEEN HOME AND CHILDCARE CENTER

Listening to and recording children's stories helps caregivers "tune in" to the thoughts and feelings of children. In the childcare center, such activities increase the bond between caregiver and child. The childcare center becomes an extension of the family home. Childcare workers know that they have made a positive impact when Kazuhiko says, "I want to live at your house," and when Stephana, a working mom, sighs and says in a sorrowful voice, "I wish I could stay here and play all day."

Shared episodes like these produce lively three-way conversations among parents, caregivers, and children. A parent hungers to know what Barry is doing all day while she is working. A childcare worker wants to know what time Barry gets to bed at night and whether his morning crankiness is related to a lack of sleep. Barry beams all over knowing that the special people in his life talk to one another about him.

Sometimes another "word" project can be used to enhance such communication. Children can dictate letters that are written down by their childcare center teacher. Following is an example.

Dear Mom,

You won't believe this, but at snack time I put my head down on the table and fell asleep. Angela [the childcare worker] said that was a good thing I did 'cause I must have really needed it. Angela told me that she goes to bed at 9:30 some nights. Can you believe it? Angela says children need lots of sleep.

Love,
Barry

Childcare centers can provide a small spiral notebook for each child to use as a handy vehicle for lively communication. The childcare worker can explain the purpose in the beginning pages. For example:

Dear Mr. and Mrs. Fernandez,

We are delighted that Barry is with us this year. Part of what we do is get to know your child well and appreciate him for his individual talents, his likes and dislikes. You can be a great help to us. You know your child better than anyone in the world! What we will do is send home this notebook to you each week, writing our own thoughts about what Barry has enjoyed doing, relationships he has made, or problems that have come up. Sometimes Barry will help us by telling us what he wants us to tell you about the fire engine puzzle he has just completed or about our new horseshoe crab.

This journal is a way for all of us to be in closer touch. For Barry, our "postman" who will carry the journal back and forth, it is a way for him to know that we all like to think and talk about him and want to help him grow.

Please write us your thoughts and questions and send them to us as often as you can. We welcome your phone calls as well, and even more important, if your time allows, we would welcome you to Barry's room whenever you care to visit.

Sincerely,
Angela and Joan

Journal-keeping can be an important piece of the educational process. An effective journal is more than a compilation of observations, questions, answers, pictures, and prose. It is even more than establishing a three-way connection. Barry's journal is a kind of extension of his baby book and the family album. It makes key child-hood information available for families, caregivers, and the child himself. It becomes a personal historical doc-ument, a visible record of a child at a particular time in his life.

Creating such a document also assists in the devel-opment of a child's self-esteem. The journal makes visible the child's accomplishments and so serves to stimulate future inquiry and experimentation. Barbara eagerly pulls her dad to see her illustration of the time they made a cardboard boat together, and the remembrance sparks a new building project. Spence grins with satis-faction as his mom reads: "Spence wants to be sure that his boat has two anchors, in case of a very bad storm." And, sure enough, the next time that Spence draws a boat, there are the two anchors!

Worthwhile additions to written and drawn journals are photographs, audiotapes, and videotapes. A field trip to a museum can be documented with snapshots that accompany the child's dictated story about the trip and his drawings of his favorite exhibits. Audiotapes can be used to record the child's thoughts throughout a given project. And videotapes can be made of group projects and performances.

Documentation in all its forms is a tool that encourages growth. Just having thoughts down on paper makes them more believable. Having drawings and paintings done by children allows for the individual points of view and shows children that the world can be seen in many different ways.

Engaging young children in words and books, whether professionally produced or handmade, recorded in journals or on tape, is perhaps the single most important thing that adults can do in preparing children for school — and, indeed, in preparing them for life.

FAVORITE CHILDREN'S BOOKS

Following are some of my favorite books to use with young children. Needless to say, they are only a few of many. Most are readily available in stores and libraries.

Arkin, Alan. *Tony's Hard Work Day*. New York: Harper & Row, 1972.

Bemelmans, Ludwig. *Madeleine*. New York: Puffin, 1977.

Blos, Joan W. *Old Henry*. New York: William Morrow, 1990.

Brown, Margaret W. *The Runaway Bunny*. New York: Harper & Row, 1942.

Brown, Margaret W. *Little Fur Family*. New York: Harper & Row, 1946.

Brown, Margaret W. *Goodnight Moon*. New York: Harper & Row, 1947.

Carle, Eric. *The Very Busy Spider*. New York: Philomel, 1984.

Carle, Eric. *The Very Hungry Caterpillar*. Cleveland: World, 1984.

Carlstrom, Nancy White. *How Does the Wind Walk?* New York: Macmillan, 1993.

Carson, Rachel. *The Sense of Wonder*. New York: Harper & Row, 1956.

Ehlert, Lois. *Red Leaf, Yellow Leaf*. New York: Harcourt Brace, 1991.

Ets, Marie Hal. *Gilberto and the Wind*. New York: Viking, 1963.

Ets, Marie Hal. *Play with Me*. New York: Viking, 1983.

Fox, Mem. *Time for Bed*. New York: Harcourt Brace, 1993.

Freeman, Don. *Corduroy*. New York: Viking, 1968.

Gans, Roma. *It's Nesting Time*. New York: Thomas Y. Crowell, 1964.

Gray, Libba Moore. *Miss Tizzy*. New York: Simon and Schuster, 1993.

Henkes, Kevin. *Chrysanthemum*. New York: Greenwillow, 1991.

Hoban, Russell. *Bread and Jam for Frances*. New York: Harper & Row, 1964.

Hoffman, Mary. *Amazing Grace*. New York: Dial, 1991.

Keats, Ezra Jack. *Peter's Chair*. New York: Harper & Row, 1967.

Keats, Ezra Jack. *A Snowy Day*. New York: Viking, 1962.

Keller, Holly. *Island Baby*. New York: Greenwillow, 1992.

Krauss, Ruth. *The Carrot Seed*. New York: Harper Collins, 1945.

Lasky, Kathryn. *Sugaring Time*. New York: Macmillan, 1986.

Leaf, Munro. *The Story of Ferdinand*. New York: Penguin, 1977.

Lionni, Leo. *Frederick*. New York: Pantheon, 1967.

Lionni, Leo. *Inch by Inch*. New York: Ivan Obolensky, 1960.

Lionni, Leo. *Swimmy*. New York: Pantheon, 1968.

Lobel, Arnold. *Frog and Toad*. New York: Harper & Row, 1972. (Series)

Mellonie, Bryan. *Lifetimes*. New York: Bantam, 1983.

Milne, A.A. *When We Were Very Young*. New York: E.P. Dutton, 1924.

Polacco, Patricia. *Thunder Cake*. New York: Philomel, 1990.

Prelutsky, Jack. *Ride a Purple Pelican*. New York: Greenwillow, 1986.

Raschka, Chris. *Yo! Yes?* New York: Orchard, 1993.

Ringold, Faith. *Tar Beach.* New York: Crown, 1991.

Rylant, Cynthia. *When I Was Young in the Mountains.* New York: E.P. Dutton, 1982.

Sendak, Maurice. *A Hole Is to Dig.* New York: Harper & Row, 1952.

Silverstein, Shel. *Where the Sidewalk Ends.* New York: Harper & Row, 1974.

Slobodkina, Esphyr. *Caps for Sale.* New York: W. R. Scott, 1940.

Thaler, Mike. *Owly.* New York: Harper & Row, 1982.

Viorst, Judith. *The Tenth Good Thing About Barney.* New York: Macmillan, 1988.

Yolen, Jane. *Owl Moon.* New York: Putnam, 1987.

Yashima, Taro. *Crow Boy.* New York: Viking, 1955.

Zolotow, Charlotte. *Mr. Rabbit and the Lovely Present.* New York: Harper & Row, 1962.

Zolotow, Charlotte. *William's Doll.* New York: Harper & Row, 1972.

CHAPTER FIVE

TELEVISION AND VIDEOS

J osiah, age three, is sitting in the corner of the couch watching television. His right thumb is in his mouth; his left thumb and forefinger are nervously working the edge of his favorite baby blanket. Josiah's mother is in the kitchen preparing chicken and rice for supper. His father is cutting back an intrusive forsythia bush just outside the back door. Daniel, Josiah's twelve-year-old brother, is playing stickball in the front street. Penrose, Josiah's eight-year-old sister, is in her bedroom diligently practicing "Song of the Wind" on her cello. Josiah is all alone in the living room as the sounds of gunshots are blasting from the TV.

What is wrong with this picture?

Josiah is in an unsafe place! No, he is not underfoot where hot pots and pans are being carried back and forth from the stove to the sink. He is not dangerously close to the pruning sheers that are rapidly snapping off the forsythia branches. He is not in the street, heedless of traffic, trying to play stickball with the big boys. Nor is he pestering Penrose to the point of exasperation. But Josiah is in a place that isn't good for him.

The scenes on the television screen make him uncomfortable and anxious. He is frightened and confused by the acts of violence that he sees. No adult is with him to monitor what he is watching, to say, "I do not want you to see this program, because it is too frightening for young children." No adult is with him to respond to his fears and questions, to explain that the guns do not fire real bullets and the "bad guys" are not really dead.

For young children, watching acts of violence is not entertainment — it is terrifying and appalling. And it is assuredly not an appropriate form of child care.

GUIDELINES FOR RESPONSIBLE VIEWING

Television and videos are here to stay. They are part of children's lives, and the impact of these visual media undoubtedly will grow even greater as more products and channels become available and programming becomes more interactive. Be that as it may, there are important things that responsible adults must do to ensure that children grow up in as "safe" an environment as possible.

Caregivers — particularly in the home and in home-centered childcare operations — need to be constantly aware of what children are watching on television. This attention cannot be confined to so-called adult programming. Caregivers also must spend time critically viewing children's programs, just as we carefully read and review children's books. High standards are important to decide how much time children should spend in front of a TV screen and what should be allowed to roll before their eager eyes and ears.

Sensible guidelines can be broadly stated:

1. Allow young children to watch television for no more than one hour a day, preferably less.

Recent studies of school-age children have established that more than three hours of TV viewing a day tends to negatively affect the quality of a child's school work. Granted, it takes more time to plan engaging projects than to say, "Go and see what's on TV." But the quality of children's lives is at stake.

2. Select television and video programs that serve specific purposes.

Walt Disney's *Pinocchio* is a perfect recipe for a rainy afternoon. Watching *Lassie Come Home* can help to while away the time when Zoe is sick and her chicken pox itch. There are excellent shows for children to watch on TV, particularly ones relating to science or nature. Caregivers should check TV listings for National Geographic shows and PBS specials.

It also is important to discuss television choices with children, just as caregivers and children discuss food choices. Making choices (from selected alternatives) helps to give young children a sense of self-sufficiency.

3. Watch television with children, rather than sending them to watch television alone.

Caregivers need to be present to monitor programs, making sure that children understand unfamiliar words and concepts and conveying their own values when they disagree with what a TV character does or says. Sometimes caregivers need to write down words that are used on television that the child may not understand and then talk about them at a commercial break. Caregivers need to challenge stereotypes that girls are "fraidy cats" or that boys always are "rough and tough."

4. Let young children know that not every television program is for them.

There will be times when adults or older children in the family will want to watch a program that is inappropriate for the young child. This is a good time for the caregiver to spend time with the child doing other things. The young child needs to learn that sometimes it is his turn to watch television and sometimes it is his brother's or sister's turn.

WHAT TO DO INSTEAD OF TELEVISION

At home, instead of filling "idle" moments with television, parents can encourage young children to engage in open-ended projects. When Kenesha finishes her breakfast, the half-hour between then and when she must leave for the childcare center might be spent making a collage. Kenesha might go to a box filled with scraps of paper and fabric, ribbons, a bottle of Elmer's glue, and a few craft sticks. Using those items along with colored construction paper, scissors, and crayons, Kenesha can transform a corner of the kitchen table that has been covered with newspaper into a tiny studio.

Another productive time comes between arriving home from the childcare center and dinnertime. Families gather at this time; meal preparation begins; older siblings start on homework assignments. What is there for the young child to do? Instead of watching television, here are some suggestions:

- Listen to Raffi's "Baby Beluga" or Shari Lewis' "Lambchop's Sing Along, Play Along" or other children's recordings.
- Draw or color using crayons and inexpensive paper or a stack of recycled office memos. Collect the pictures in a folder.
- Play with clay or homemade art dough. Set aside a small table or a section of kitchen counter.
- Use old magazines, scissors, and paste to construct a scrapbook around a certain theme, such as cars or animals.
- Make a space to one side of the kitchen sink so that the child can "prepare supper" using a bowl of soapsuds and a wooden spoon.
- Keep an old photo album handy for browsing.

These and similar activities allow children to be close by but not under foot. They can join in discussions and talk about their day without interfering with necessary household tasks.

TELEVISION AND CHILDCARE CENTERS

This chapter has focused on television and video use in the home because I firmly believe that television does not have a place at childcare centers that serve children five or younger.

Childcare centers should be lively places where caregivers provide imaginative materials for youngsters in every inch of the room. Such centers are places where Tyrene and Carolyn can work together, gingerly changing the guinea pig's cage. They are places where children can shape dough into pretzels for a make-believe business.

Childcare centers should be filled with noisy and quiet, challenging and exhilarating experiences for young children. They should be filled with talking, joking, laughing, singing, reading, rhyming, painting, building, role playing, experimenting, tugging, hugging, running, jumping, swinging, sliding, risking, resolving, reflecting, caring, trusting, and loving.

In such an environment, television is not merely superfluous, it is intrusive.

CHAPTER SIX

OUTDOOR EXPLORATION

To plant a single pumpkin seed in the garden and watch it grow, to dig in the earth and uncover one very wiggly redworm, to gaze at a spider on a tree branch as it spins an intricate web, to catch snowflakes on the tongue, to watch a hummingbird sip nectar from the crimson phlox, to catch a flashing firefly in a jelly jar — a whole wide world is waiting for young children just outside the door.

Caregivers will find their spirits uplifted by the wonder of discovery that young children exhibit when they begin to explore the outdoors. While children learn much about the outdoors from indoor activities such as planting a bean in a paper cup filled with soil, so much more awaits their attention in the world outside.

The caregiver's job is twofold: 1) to go outdoor exploring with children as often as possible and 2) to create circumstances in which children can make their own discoveries.

It is not difficult to find time to go outdoors if caregivers make such activities a priority. And creating opportunities for discovery is relatively simple. Caregivers will have a supply of pumpkin seeds for spring planting simply by drying and saving the seeds from one fall jack o'lantern. Old metal spoons are perfectly satisfactory implements for children to dig in the earth in search of wiggly redworms.

Mother, father, grandparent, or sibling can join the fun of staying up late with the young child to run through the grass in pursuit of fireflies that, when caught in a jelly jar, punctuate the darkness with their captive light.

Whatever caregivers choose to do outdoors may broaden the child's experience. And how much more wholesome that form of experience is when adults and children slip on jeans, grab a bag of trail mix, and head for a park, rather than piling into the car for a shopping spree at the mall.

PREPARING FOR OUTDOOR EXPLORATION

One way for adults to think about outdoor exploration for young children is to recall their own childhood experiences in the outdoors. What was it like to look for crawdads in the sunlit stream just down the road? Or to collect fall leaves along the sidewalk? Or to grow parsley in an old yogurt container on the window sill? What was it like to watch the stars from the apartment roof or lying down in a field with wild blueberries all around?

Caregivers need to think like children, in simple unlayered thoughts. They need to feel, see, hear, taste, and smell things directly in their simplest forms. Before an adult can teach a child to explore natural things, he needs to explore in childlike ways, examining a single birch leaf, front and back, running his fingers over the bumpy edges and along the stem, holding it up to the light to see its veins. The warm dry sand must slip through his fingers over and over again. He must bury his nose in the lilac bush and breathe the perfume. He must gather blueberries warmed by the sun and immediately pop them into his mouth.

Wonderful things can happen when adults and children explore outdoors and do these things. Such simple pursuits bring great calm and a sense of satisfaction. These are moments to share with youngsters, to feel a connectedness both to them and to the earth.

Of course, it is much easier for people who live in the country to spend a large amount of time outdoors exploring fields and woods. But restless, bustling cities also hold many outdoor fascinations. Caregivers in city settings still need to pause for a moment when the child reaches out to catch a shaft of light that glances between two tall buildings. They need to pause when the toddler bends to examine a crack in the sidewalk or to walk three times around a red and yellow fire hydrant.

The sky is a common denominator. Clouds of different types float overhead, transforming the sky and the light from moment to moment. Clouds are a favorite source of wonderment. They can be viewed "scientifically" and discussed in terms of rain and snow. Or they can be seen as characters from stories, this one a dragon, that one a field mouse. And just before bedtime, when the clouds part, there are stars to count and wonder at.

Caregivers must realize that young children need to develop a kinship with the outdoors as a natural way of encouraging broader exploration and to build their self-confidence. Caregivers should arouse the emotions of young children, so that they are eager and enthusiastic about what they see and do outdoors. It is not necessary to provide scientific or botanical names or to attempt to fill young children's heads with facts. Young children do delight in learning new words like *hibernation, cumulus,* or even *metamorphosis,* as long as it is done in a lighthearted way. But what caregivers should keep in mind is the goal of kindling that sense of kinship to a single "froggy pond," a single garden plot, a single potted pumpkin seed, or a piece of sky.

Caregivers who provide time and opportunities for outdoor exploration foster the love of discovery. They awaken a sense of wonder in children. That should be the goal. The rest will blossom of its own accord.

BRINGING OUTDOOR LESSONS INSIDE

Many of the "products" of outdoor exploration can be brought into the home or childcare center. Collecting fall leaves as an outdoor activity leads to looking for similarities and differences among the leaves. Children can sort the leaves by sizes, shapes, colors, or vein patterns. From looking at broad expanses of nature outdoors, children can begin to look at natural objects more closely, rejoicing in their details, when they bring their collections indoors.

Children can scout for acorns, pine cones, moss, stones, and plants to make a terrarium. They can dig up several buckets of earth to bring inside for making habitats or for planting seeds while the earth is frozen. And then, when the spring thaw comes, they can take their seedlings out to the garden and plant them.

Children can dig for earthworms to bring inside to make a "worm farm" in a clear plastic storage box. John and Marcia can scoop up ants for an "ant farm" and then observe the ants at work. They can bring in bittersweet and watch the berries pop open and change color. They can collect dry grasses and seed pods to put in vases to remember the look of fall now that snow blankets the meadows.

Collecting natural objects also can give children a sense of purpose as they walk the same "path" twice a week on the way to the laundromat or to the grocery. Indeed, there is something to be said for walking the same "path" over and over again throughout the whole year. Then Bertram can spot the first golden crocus that pokes its head through the last blanket of snow in the spring. He can marvel at the dazzling blossom, watch as the flower fades, and then notice that the crocuses are replaced by summer flowers. In the fall he can watch the green leaves turn to yellow and brown. From such observations Bertram will come to understand the cycles of nature and how the seasons change the world around him.

SEASONS OF PLAY AND LEARNING

Children need to spend worlds of time outside in all kinds of weather. How else will Edmond discover what heat and cold and snow are all about? Just being outside is different from being inside in many ways. The space outside is usually larger than the indoor area. There is room for John to run, kick a ball, swing a bat,

and feel what his body can do. Outside is the place where Marcia can turn a cartwheel (almost) and shout at the top of her lungs.

Outside is a place to let go, where Samuel can swoop down the slide and then run lickety-split around to the ladder so that he can swoop down again. Even the air outside is different. It is more refreshing, more invigo-rating. It gives children (and adults) a surge of power. And the outside light is different. Natural light is easier on the senses. There are no flickering fluorescent bulbs to play on the nerves. Outside children can see the real colors of the vibrant bittersweet vine that entangles the locust tree or the dull black macadam that covers the parking lot.

Outdoor exploration and indoor learning and play are natural companions at home or in a childcare cen-ter. Many activities can be carried out even when the "official" outdoor play area is only a small yard. Here are a few activity ideas that follow the seasons.

Fall. Children can rake fallen leaves into enormous piles in which to jump and frolic. After their play, they can gather interesting leaves to bring inside to study.

Children can explore a nearby stream, perhaps tak-ing long sticks to clear out leaves and rocks to allow the water to run more freely. Remembering the stream, they can talk about building bridges and draw pictures that recall their exploration.

Using yarn and cardboard tubes from toilet paper rolls, children can construct make-believe binoculars to carry along on nature walks, the better to spot bluejays and cardinals or to count the pigeons that roost on the ledges of buildings.

Winter. New things are ripe for discovery when cold weather sets in. The same nature walk reveals changes in the trees and plants. Thomas can try to put his trowel in the dirt and discover that it is frozen.

Children can build a feeding station, bringing to it pine cones gathered in the fall that they have now filled

with peanut butter and bird seed. Or they can hang suet in small net bags and watch from the window to see what kinds of birds come to eat their offerings.

Children can make freezing and thawing experiments, putting water in various shaped containers, such as muffin tins and pie pans.

JoAnn can make a snow sculpture and work on it right in the sink, using snow brought inside in a big soup pot.

Children can write books describing their snow experiences and experiments. Pictures and collages make great illustrations.

Making snow angels in new-fallen snow can be followed by reading Ezra Jack Keats' book, *A Snowy Day*.

Spring. When the days are sunny and the nights are cool, children can hang sap buckets on a maple tree and watch the sap begin to flow. Collecting the sap each morning to bring inside and gently boil on the stove can culminate with eating pancakes topped with the children's own maple syrup. Children can read Kathryn Lasky's *Sugaring Time.*

A small plot of land can be made into Steve's garden, where he plants cantaloupe, carrot, and zinnia seeds while wearing a straw hat and a red bandanna. Ruth Kraus' *The Carrot Seed* makes a good reading to complement this activity.

Children can hang a mesh bag filled with pieces of yarn and string, paper, cotton, feathers, fur, animal hair, or strips of bright fabric poking through the holes so that birds can use the materials to make nests.

Warm weather can be a good time to take easels, paints, and brushes out to the open air. Let Lawrence and Max be like the impressionist artists, as they paint a picture of their favorite scene.

Summer. Claire and Benjamin can bring out a tub of soapy water and an old-fashioned scrubbing board to wash doll dresses. A miniature clothesline of wrapping cord can be strung between two nearby trees.

Warm weather is the time to haul out old funnels, pipes, and faucets to let Ricardo and Gabrielle take turns doing water experiments with buckets and pitchers.

Pails of water and wide brushes, brought out into the sunshine, can transform Jerry and Hugh into artists who can paint the outside walls and fences.

Outdoors, instead of indoors, can become the central space for story time, snack time, lunch time, and play time.

Being outdoors with young children is a cause for jubilation, a time for boundless liberation of body and soul. Caregivers who discover the joys of working with young children in outdoor exploration will find new activities at every turn.

CHAPTER SEVEN

FINDING QUALITY CHILD CARE

"I have such mixed feelings about choosing child care, as I know I am the only one who really knows my Gloria and can do the absolute best job of taking care of her."

"I feel both cheated and guilty that I can't stay home with my kid. This is what I always dreamed of. I can't bear to think of Trevor taking his first wobbly steps to go to someone else."

These are among the comments I have heard from the parents of young children. Perhaps the hardest part of selecting child care for Gloria and Trevor is working through all the nagging emotions of not being able to stay home to personally care for one's child.

Most parents need to work to support their families, and fewer families in our modern era can afford a stay-at-home adult to care for young children. But no single type of care is best for every family. Some families can provide direct care for some or most of every day; others depend on babysitters and childcare centers to take care of their children for most of the children's waking hours.

Part of selecting satisfactory child care is recognizing that this wide range of care needs is now reflected in an equally wide range of care options. Thus choosing the "right" option has become a primary concern.

THREE OPTIONS

If members of the immediate family are not available to care for the child, then one of the following options may be the "right" one.

Extended Family. One choice may be to call on members of one's extended family if they are nearby and willing and able to take on the childcare responsibilities. This can be a comforting solution, as parents are dealing with a trusted person — aunt, uncle, brother, grandmother — who already knows and loves their child.

Home Care. Another option, so that Gloria can stay in the surroundings she knows best, where her Peter Cottontail is waiting for her on her bed and where she can parade around in her cuddly pink bathrobe whenever she feels the need, is home care.

Home care means employing a carefully chosen, well-qualified individual who will come into the home to care for the child while the parents or guardians are away. However, home care often is quite expensive and therefore beyond the means of many families.

Childcare Center. For most parents who need childcare, a group situation is the "right" option. Childcare centers range from small-scale, home-based centers for a few children to large-scale, commercial centers that enroll many children and offer services that begin with infant care and extend through full-day kindergarten.

CRITERIA FOR CHOOSING A CHILDCARE SETTING

Parents and guardians seeking childcare must consider convenience — location, hours, etc. — and affordability. But above these qualities, they must seek child care that is best for their child in terms of the *quality of interactions between caregivers and children.*

Because a child often must be taken to the childcare center before the parent goes to work and picked up after the workday ends, she actually spends a longer day "at work" than the parent does. Consequently, a childcare setting must be chosen that will make those long hours stimulating, fulfilling, and satisfying.

A recommendation from a trusted friend regarding a childcare center is certainly helpful. Pamphlets con-

taining lists of goals and standards and glossy photographs are useful, too. But nothing substitutes for
spending time in potential childcare rooms while caregivers and children go about their regular activities. This
practice is especially useful if the child can join in on a
trial basis.

Following are 18 questions that may help in the eval-
uation of a potential childcare setting:

1. Do the children in the center appear to be comfortable and relaxed? During a trial period, does
   the new child readily join in activities? (Keep in
   mind that many children need time to adjust to
   new situations.)
2. Are the interactions between caregiver and children pleasant and respectful? Does the caregiver greet each child kindly and enthusiastically?
   Do the children appear eager to share ideas
   and talk with the caregiver?
3. Does the caregiver use positive, specific language to encourage children, such as saying to
   a child, "I like the way you have created a pattern by using three red pieces and then adding
   two white ones on top of that."
4. Does the caregiver's voice convey warmth,
   enthusiasm, and understanding in interactions
   with children, both in groups and individually?
5. In group activities, is the caregiver able to su-
   pervise the entire group and still make time for
   individual children?
6. In a setting where two or more adults work
   together with children, do the adults seem to
   enjoy working with one another? Do they talk
   easily among themselves, thus modeling friend-
   ly, cooperative interactions for the children? Do
   they work as a team?
7. Do children engage in many different activities,
   both quiet and noisy, singly and in pairs or

small groups in various areas of the room? Are individual needs being met, rather than all children doing the same thing at the same time?

8. Are there challenging activities from which to choose, such as:
   - art activities (paper, paint, clay, etc.)?
   - science activities (sand and water table, ant farm, etc.)?
   - building activities (blocks of various types and sizes)?
   - make-believe activities (toy cars, kitchen utensils, etc.)?
   - physical activities (balls, swings, etc.)?
   - language activities (storybooks, posters, poems, computer, etc.)?

9. Does the caregiver promptly intervene in problem situations or does she give the children time to work it out themselves? Is discipline handled in nonpunitive ways that respect each child's individuality and feelings?

10. When the child has a hard time saying good-bye to the parent, does the caregiver give special attention to drawing the child into the day's activities?

11. Is the physical environment appropriate to the children's development? Are infant rooms quiet, soothing places? Are rooms for two- and three-year-olds distinguished from rooms for four- and five-year-olds by books and materials that are best for each age?

12. How do the children respond to their environment? Do children freely express themselves with words and through their body movements, yet show respect for one another (and for their caregivers)?

13. Are caregivers safety-conscious? Is playground equipment kept in good repair, free from exposed nails and splinters? Are toys and books well-maintained? Are the children encouraged to treat materials with respect and to help repair the broken legs of the wooden policeman or the post for the red-and-white stop sign?

14. Is cleanliness emphasized? What happens when four-year-old Rick spills his orange juice on the snack table? Are there sponges on the table and a child-size mop nearby so that he can easily handle the situation by himself? Are hazardous materials (such as commercial cleaning products) stored out of a child's reach or kept under lock and key?

15. Are clear emergency procedures in place? Are the phone numbers of parents and each child's pediatrician maintained and up to date? Are staff members trained in first aid and CPR? Is the first-aid kit close at hand?

16. Is the ratio of caregivers to children appropriate? A rule of thumb for infants is one caregiv-

er for every three children; for two's, one to four; for three's, one to six; for four's and five's, one to eight.

17. Are parents welcome to visit and participate in activities with their children?

18. Are the meals provided to children balanced and nutritious? Meals should take into consideration children's preferences so that nutritious food is not left uneaten. Also, childcare providers must be familiar with any special food needs, including food allergies, that must be accommodated.

At the end of this chapter, parents will find a handy checklist that incorporates these points.

PARENTS AND CHILD CARE

Parents can play an important role at child-care centers in enhancing their children's success and, in so doing, can fulfill their own need to be involved in their children's care and learning. Caregivers and parents need to consider themselves as close partners in educating young children. A child's positive development is greatly enhanced by the quality and degree of involvement that parents can provide. Interest counts for a lot.

If Hayden's dad can visit for a few minutes in the morning and watch his son put on the busman's cap and take an imaginary ride to Grandview Park, he is sharing his child's world in a significant way. If Hayden's dad can get off work to join the children's group on a field trip to watch linguini being made, he is fostering meaningful connections between himself and his son and Hayden's caregivers.

Parents also can offer the children's childcare center or other care providers new and fresh ideas that can be incorporated into the children's play and learning activities. Such ideas may come from their perspectives on their own children or from such other sources as their professional experiences or academic study.

Parents need to be certain to choose a childcare setting in which they are viewed as important partners in their children's education. Is the staff patient and fair-minded in its dealings with parents? Do caregivers find time to talk with parents often, not just when there is a problem? What voice do parents have in the childcare center's procedures and curriculum? How often are parent meetings scheduled? What resources does the center provide to guide parents in working effectively with their children?

By attending to the questions posed in this chapter, parents and guardians can ensure that the childcare setting in which they place their trust is healthy, affirming, and responsive to the social, emotional, and developmental needs of their young children.

CHILDCARE SETTING OBSERVATION CHECKLIST

Rate each characteristic when you visit a potential childcare setting.

	Most of the time	Sometimes	Seldom	Not done/ Not observed
1. Children appear to be comfortable and relaxed.	☐	☐	☐	☐
2. Interactions between caregivers and children are pleasant and respectful.	☐	☐	☐	☐
3. Caregivers use positive, specific praise and encouragement.	☐	☐	☐	☐
4. Caregivers convey warmth and enthusiasm when speaking to children.	☐	☐	☐	☐
5. Caregivers provide satisfactory group and individual supervision.	☐	☐	☐	☐
6. Caregivers and other adults in the childcare setting model friendliness and co-operation.	☐	☐	☐	☐
7. Children can work in groups, pairs, and individually.	☐	☐	☐	☐
8. Children engage in many different activities, both quiet and noisy. Check the kinds of activities that you observe:	☐	☐	☐	☐
☐ art activities (paper, paint, clay, etc.)	☐	☐	☐	☐
☐ science activities (sand and water table, ant farm, etc.)	☐	☐	☐	☐
☐ building activities (blocks of various types and sizes, etc.)	☐	☐	☐	☐
☐ make-believe activities (toy cars, kitchen utensils, etc.)	☐	☐	☐	☐
☐ physical activities (balls, swings, climbers, etc.)	☐	☐	☐	☐
☐ language activities (storybooks, poems, etc.)	☐	☐	☐	☐

	Most of the time	Sometimes	Seldom	Not done/ Not observed
9. Caregivers intervene promptly when problems arise.	☐	☐	☐	☐
10. Caregivers discipline children in non-punitive ways.	☐	☐	☐	☐
11. Caregivers give special attention to children on days that they have a hard time saying good-bye to the parent.	☐	☐	☐	☐
12. The physical environment is appropriate to the age and developmental needs of the children.	☐	☐	☐	☐
13. Children express themselves freely but show respect for one another.	☐	☐	☐	☐
14. Cleanliness is emphasized.	☐	☐	☐	☐
15. The center has clear emergency procedures.	☐	☐	☐	☐
16. The center maintains up-to-date records of parents' phone numbers and the phone numbers of each child's pediatrician.	☐	☐	☐	☐
17. Staff members are trained in first aid and CPR.	☐	☐	☐	☐
18. A first-aid kit is readily available in each room of the childcare center.	☐	☐	☐	☐
19. The ratio of caregivers to children is appropriate for the ages of the children.	☐	☐	☐	☐
20. Parents are welcome to visit and participate in activities with their children.	☐	☐	☐	☐
21. Appetizing and nutritious meals are provided that take into consideration children's tastes and preferences.	☐	☐	☐	☐
22. Teachers accommodate children's special food needs.	☐	☐	☐	☐

Children are the magic in our lives. They make difficult hours bearable by their infectious smiles and trusting looks. When their eyes sparkle, so do ours. More often than not, children bring out the best we have to offer. They make us laugh. And with their small hand in ours, they can set us skipping along a sidewalk or racing down a hill.

Children can make us sing silly songs, swing on swings, play hide-and-seek, and take picnics in the park. They allow us — make us —recapture the joys we knew when we were very young.

Children also are our deepest concern. It is for them that we "childproof" the apartment, putting the aspirin on the highest shelf out of Mary's reach. It is for them that we try never to run out of milk and bananas, because we want their young bodies to grow healthy and strong. It is for them that we squirrel away quarters, saving up for their first iridescent blue tricycle. It is for them that we think deeply about the very best things to do for our children — and then try hard to do them.

Nurturing young children is the most important job that we can ever have. We who are caregivers — parents, step-parents, guardians, grandparents, childcare providers, friends, and neighbors — must be the bedrock of our land. We are responsible for the future.

We must see that our children are healthy, rested, and fit. We must establish the first warm and steadfast relationships that allow children to feel secure in themselves and in their world. We must provide the safe environments in which children are free to play. And we must maintain the learning climate, providing well-ordered spaces where curiosity and creativity are rewarded with frequent, specific praise. We must listen to children and respect their thoughts. We must read them poetry and picture books and tell them fascinating stories.

We must take our children outdoors to feel the warmth of the sun, to make their first snowballs, to pick their first bouquet of golden dandelions, and to see and hear the bustling streets of their neighborhood.

Is our job hard work? Of course! Does it demand our best? Almost always. Does it ask more than we think we can do? Often. But the rewards are great, for by working with young children we discover ourselves and dream the future.

HELPFUL BOOKS FOR PARENTS AND CAREGIVERS

Balaban, Nancy. *Learning to Say Goodbye*. New York: Penguin, 1987.

Barnouw, Elsa. *Adventures with Children*. New York: Agathon, 1986.

Brazelton, T. Berry. *Touchpoints*. Reading, Mass.: Addison-Wesley, 1992.

Dombro, Amy Laura. *The Ordinary Is Extraordinary*. New York: Simon and Schuster, 1988.

Dombro, Amy Laura. *Sharing the Caring*. New York: Simon and Schuster, 1991.

Edelman, Marian Wright. *The Measure of Our Success*. Boston: Beacon, 1992.

Elkind, David. *Understanding Your Child*. Needham Heights, Mass.: Paramount, 1994.

Galinsky, Ellen. *The Preschool Years*. New York: Random House, 1988.

Greenman, Jim. *Caring Spaces, Learning Places: Children's Environments that Work*. Redmond, Wash.: Exchange, 1988.

Greenspan, Stanley. *The Essential Partnership*. New York: Viking, 1989.

Kutner, Lawrence. *Parent and Child*. New York: Avon, 1991.

LeShan, Eda. *When Your Child Drives You Crazy*. New York: St. Martin's, 1985.

Spock, Benjamin. *A Better World for Our Children*. Bethesda, Md.: National, 1994.

Turecki, Stanley. *The Difficult Child*. New York: Bantam, 1989.